W9-DIG-024

Published by Creative Education
123 South Broad Street, Mankato, Minnesota 56001
Creative Education is an imprint of The Creative Company

Designed by Stephanie Blumenthal
Production Design by Melinda Belter and Rose Preble

Photographs by Anthony Dalton, Nancy Ferguson, Galyn C. Hammond, Dick
Hemingway, Paul McMahon, Diane Meyer, James E. Proctor III,
Tom Stack & Associates, Videogram Communications

Library of Congress Cataloging-in-Publication Data

Richardson, Adele, 1966–
Money / by Adele Richardson
p. cm. — (Let's Investigate)
Includes index and glossary
Summary: Provides simple history of money as it replaced bartering, explains
how some types of money are used, and shows how things such as checks and
credit cards serve as invisible money.
ISBN 0-88682-555-5
1. Money—Juvenile literature. 2. Saving and investment—Juvenile literature. 3. Finance, Personal—Juvenile
literature. [1. Money. 2. Saving and investment. 3. Finance, personal.] I. Title. II. Series. III. Series: Let's
Investigate (Mankato, Minn.)
HG222.5.R53   1999
332.024—dc21   98-36407

First edition

2 4 6 8 9 7 5 3 1

MONEY

ADELE RICHARDSON

Creative C Education

MONEY
PIGGY

The first piggy banks, made in the 14th century, were made of clay and had to be broken to get the money out.

Money is important to people all over the world. It's used to buy food, clothing, cars, games—just about anything. Its appearance and **value** change depending on the country in which it is made, but one thing's for sure—we all need it!

Below, piggy bank Right, latest style of the U.S. 100-dollar bill

FEDERAL RESERVE N

AB 04443813
B2

UNITED STATES · FEDERAL RESERVE SYSTEM ·

THIS NOTE IS LEGAL TENDER
FOR ALL DEBTS, PUBLIC AND PRIVATE

Treasurer of the United States.

E2

100

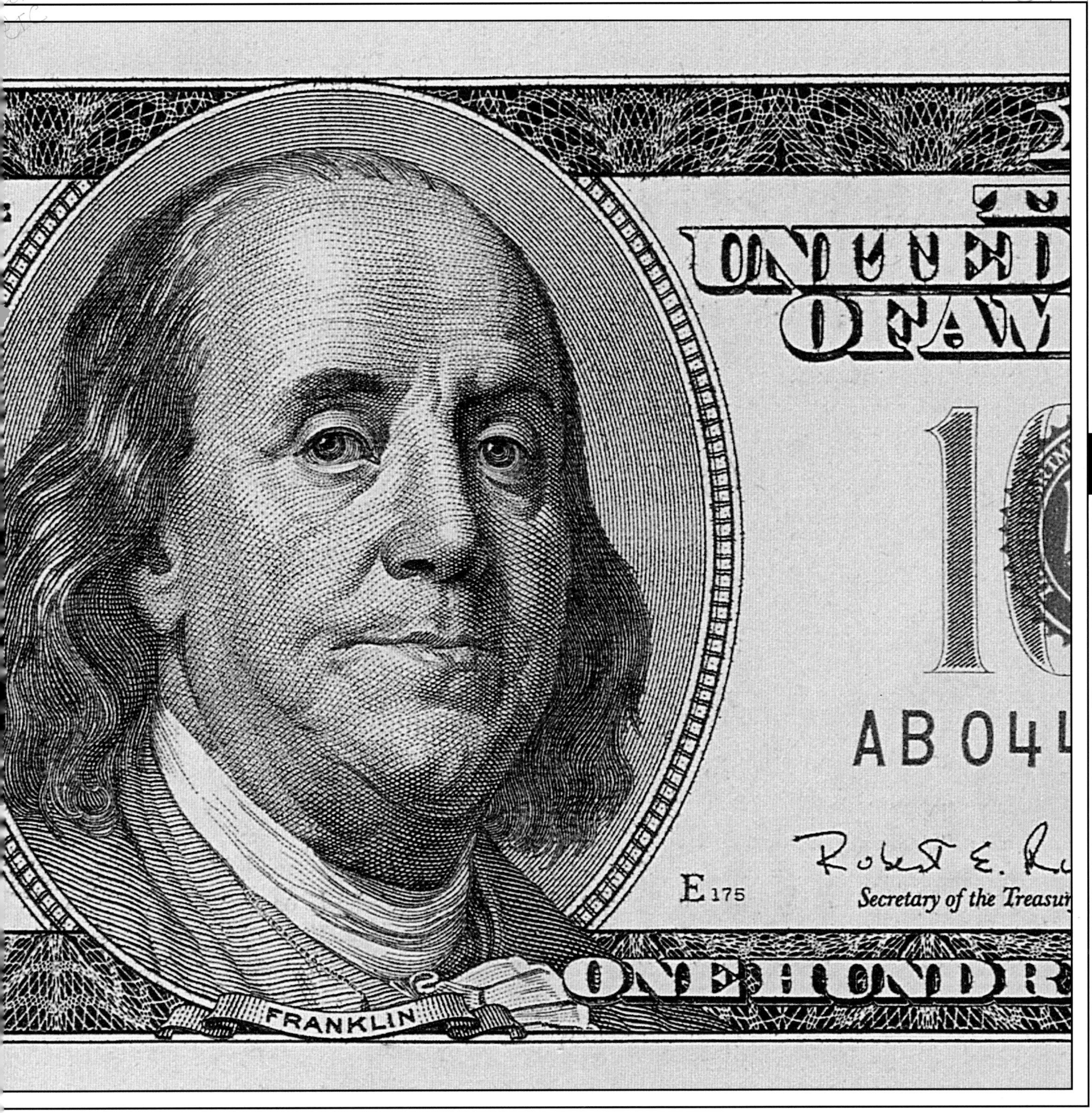
E 175
FRANKLIN

MONEY

N A M E

A quarter is named after its value—one quarter, or one-fourth, of a dollar.

6

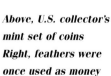

Above, U.S. collector's mint set of coins
Right, feathers were once used as money

Before money was invented, people couldn't just go to a store and buy something. They had to trade the things they owned for other things they wanted or needed. This practice is called **bartering**. In order for bartering to work, the objects two people are offering must be of some value. For example, a farmer who grew grain might trade with someone who raised chickens. This way both families could have grain to make bread, and meat to cook.

Bartering was never limited to trading just foods. A person who made blankets might find lots of people to barter with when the weather turned cold. Others may offer to trade for food or clothing. For example, a person who knew how to build a barn would be very valuable to someone who raised cows.

MONEY
A G E

The Italian culture has a long tradition of using money; in fact, the first banks were opened up in Italy during the 1500s.

MONEY
H O B B Y

People who collect coins as a hobby are called numismatists. Some old, rare coins are worth thousands of dollars.

Nails were also once used as money

7

8

Trading things back and forth is not as easy as it sounds. Many times the value of an object is different for each person, depending on what his or her needs and wants are. Having no one to trade with would be a problem. An orange grower certainly wouldn't want to trade with another orange grower. If no one else wanted his oranges, the fruit would be left to spoil, becoming worthless. People felt that there had to be a better way.

Bartering still takes place at markets around the world

The U.S. Treasury will replace a partially damaged or torn bill as long as the bearer has a little more than half of it.

9

Left, blocks of salt once used as money
Below, solid gold bars

BETTER THAN TRADE

After people began to realize how hard bartering could be, many villages developed a **medium of exchange**. This is where a group of people agree on the value of an object and use it as payment for goods or services. Depending on the culture, a medium of exchange can be a piece of gold, a goat or sheep, or even stones.

MONEY

A one-dollar bill in the U.S. lasts for an average of 18 months before it's worn out.

Below, chickens were often bartered
Right, coins from countries in Asia

The ancient Chinese used smooth shells found in warm water oceans, called cowrie shells, as money. In Mongolia and western Asia, tea was very valuable. It was made into bricks and used as a form of money. In Africa, blocks of salt were considered forms of money. Other items used for money around the world were used seeds, beads, livestock, and feathers.

There was still a problem though. Many of these mediums of exchange could be easily damaged. A shell can break. A cow might get sick. Seeds and feathers may blow away. Food could spoil—or be eaten! People needed something small, valuable, and tough as a medium of exchange. The answer to this problem was metal money.

11

Below, animals are often depicted on currency

MONEY
BUNDLE

12

Above, the U.S. Mint in Denver, Colorado Lower right, early Chinese coins

CREATING METAL MONEY

There's no special place or time in history proving when metal money was first used. Some believe it was over 5,000 years ago in Mesopotamia. We do know that the people of Greece made and used coins around 700 B.C. These were gold, silver, and bronze **nuggets** flattened and stamped with a picture or a design. This was tough work because each coin had to be stamped by hand with a hammer.

The type of money that is used the most all around the world is the U.S. dollar.

13

Today, money is made by machines in **mints** using less valuable materials than gold and silver. Melted metals are poured and rolled into sheets. After the metal hardens, the shapes of the coins are punched out of the sheet and stamped with the proper design. Pennies and nickels (in U.S. money) are polished and sent through a machine that gives them a raised rim. Dollar coins, quarters, and dimes are milled coins. This means their edges have rough ridges. These also go through special machines that do all the work.

Early European coins— gold and silver—found by treasure hunters in a Pacific Ocean shipwreck

MONEY

It's a law in the United States that the design of a coin be kept for at least 25 years.

MONEY

EUROPE

The Euro, the unified currency of 11 European countries, became legal money January 1, 1999, though the actual coins and bills wouldn't be used until 2002.

Right, U.S. quarters and dimes have milled edges Opposite, money being counted and wrapped by automatic machines

The invention of metal money allowed for a less confusing medium of exchange than feathers or seeds, but it too had problems. If a person carried too much, the coins could be very heavy. This problem was solved with the creation of paper money.

The U.S. island of Manhattan, now one of the world's most valuable pieces of land, was traded in 1626 for 24 dollars worth of beads.

BANK NOTES

The Chinese were the first people known to use paper money. This was sometime around 1300. Most paper money as we know it was made in the 1700s in the form of **bank notes**. Bank notes were issued by many small banks and business owners all over the world. They were promises to pay money to the customer in exchange for the note.

Front (top) and back (bottom) of an old Chinese bank note

Front (top) and back (bottom) of an old U.S. five-dollar bank note

The problem with bank notes was that sometimes the banks didn't have enough gold and silver to pay for the notes. Other times, one bank would not accept notes from another bank. Notes could be worth anywhere from three cents to hundreds of dollars, and they were very easy to **counterfeit**. Even this was a confusing medium of exchange.

MONEY CODE

Letters on the right side of the faces on U.S. coins can tell you where they were made: Denver (D), New Orleans (O), Philadelphia (P), or San Francisco (S).

18

Above, the tiny "D" on this coin indicates that it was minted in Denver. Right, old U.S. bank note.

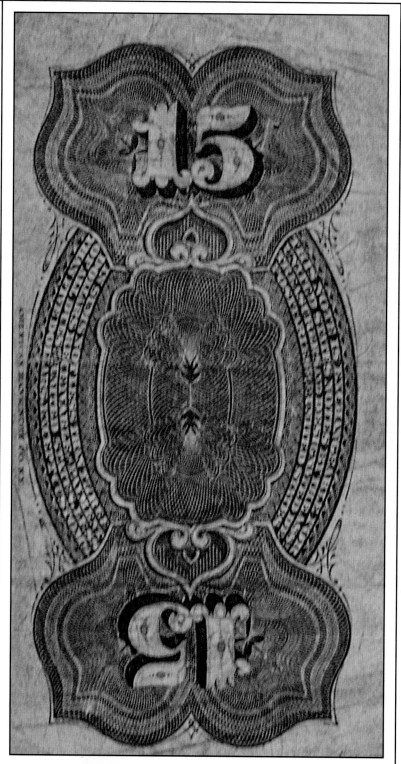

In 1861, the United States government decided to stop the practice of bank notes and print their own paper money, which they called greenbacks. These bills earned their name because their backs were printed in green ink. Some banks were still allowed to issue **currency**, but by 1877 the government had stopped the practice.

FAKE MONEY

Ever since money was first created, there have been people all over the world who have tried to make more of it by counterfeiting, or creating fake copies. This is one reason milled coins were invented; milling is very hard for counterfeiters to duplicate.

MONEY
DONUT

From 1813 to 1822, dollar coins in New South Wales, Australia, were made with a hole in the middle. The cut from the middle, called a "dump," could also be used as money.

MONEY
MICRO

The smallest money ever used, called an obelas, was made in Greece. One obelas was smaller than an apple seed.

Chinese money

MONEY

FACT

All paper money made in the U.S. is printed in Washington, D.C., at the Bureau of Engraving and Printing.

Below, an antique cash register
Center, U.S. currency shows various historic buildings, including Independence Hall

Counterfeiting is a crime in every country of the world. During the 1800s, people could be hanged in England if they were caught with fake currency. Today, in the United States, a counterfeiter may end up in jail for 15 years and have to pay a fine of $5,000.

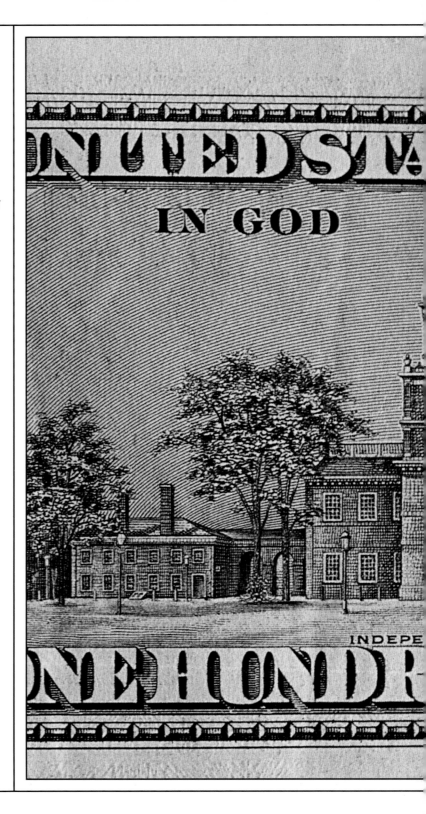

By using special paper and ink for printing their money, many countries make it hard for criminals to copy money. Usually the ink and paper are secret recipes that can only be used by a country's government. Sometimes a "watermark" is used. A watermark is a special mark made in the paper money is printed on. When a bill is held up to a light, the mark can be seen. In the U.S., when bills worth 20 dollars or more are held up to a light, a thin magnetic strip can be seen embedded in the paper.

The Latin phrase e pluribus unum means "from many, one." It was chosen in 1776 for the Great Seal of the United States and relates to the nation being formed from the 13 original colonies.

One Greek drachma

MONEY
MATTERS

By law all coins in the United States must show the date they were made and have the word "Liberty" on them.

MONEY
BIRTHDAY

U.S. pennies with Abraham Lincoln on the front were first made in 1909, the 100th anniversary of Lincoln's birthday.

Today, money is made by automatic machines

EXCHANGING MONEY FOR MONEY

All the countries around the world have different currency. While some currencies may have the same name (both Canada and the U.S. have dollars), they are of different values. Whenever people travel to another country, they must exchange their money for the currency that is used in the country they are visiting. Large banks and airports around the world usually have a place where these exchanges can be made.

MONEY
S I Z E

Yap is the heaviest money ever used. Made of stone, a Yap can weigh more than 500 pounds (225 kg) and measure 12 feet (4 m) tall.

MONEY
B I T S

A quarter is sometimes called "two bits" because old Spanish dollar coins could be cut up into eight pieces. Two pieces—or bits— equaled one quarter of a dollar.

Paper currency from around the world

A traveler can get an idea of what their money is worth in another country by looking at the foreign exchange rate listed in many major newspapers and available at any bank. This rate changes often, so what U.S. money is worth in Mexico one day will probably be a little different the next week.

MONEY
PHRASE

The phrase "In God We Trust" began appearing on U.S. coins and currency April 22, 1864.

Country and currency	One unit equals this in U.S. dollars	One U.S. dollar equals this in other units
Australian dollar	$ 0.56	1.80 dollars
British pound	$ 1.65	.61 pounds
Canadian dollar	$ 0.63	1.58 dollars
Japanese yen	$ 0.007	1775.00 yen
Mexican peso	$ 0.10	9.92 pesos

Coin designs vary from nation to nation

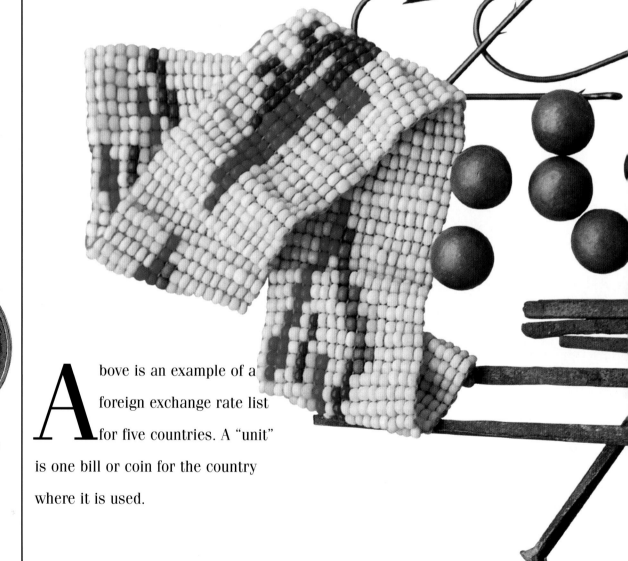

Above is an example of a foreign exchange rate list for five countries. A "unit" is one bill or coin for the country where it is used.

or example, if a person were visiting Japan and wanted to buy a souvenir costing 1,200 yen, the price could be figured in U.S. money. This is done by multiplying the price of the souvenir (1,200 yen) by the amount listed in the first column (.007 cents). In American money, the souvenir would cost $8.40.

The reason the foreign exchange rate changes is because a country's economy changes everyday. For example, if the U.S. buys more goods and services from Mexico, the value of the peso will go up, so the U.S. dollar will not be worth as much in that country.

MONEY
TOOLS

Some early Chinese coins were made of bronze and formed into the shapes of tools such as knives and shovels.

Beadwork, musket balls, fishing hooks, nails, and raw silver were all once used as money in various countries

MONEY

SECRET

U.S. bills are printed with a secret formula ink that never completely dries.

MONEY

FACT

The unit of money in Germany, called the mark, was first issued in 1871. One mark is equal to 100 pfennigs in Germany.

Money from France (right) and from Czechoslovakia (opposite)

INVISIBLE MONEY

Money is more than coins and paper. Sometimes money is never seen or touched. This medium of exchange is called **credit,** and it is a way to borrow money.

Credit cards work like money. A company that issues a credit card to a person agrees to pay for all the purchases made with the card. They pay the store electronically, meaning that a computer transfers the money from their bank account to the store's account. No money is ever actually handled by people.

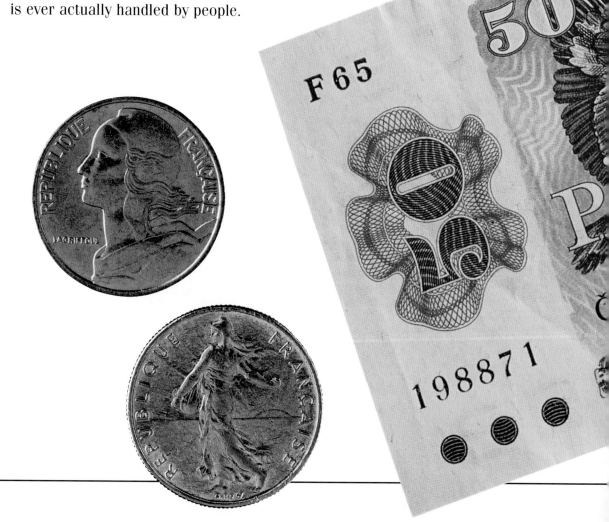

MONEY

FACT

In 1685 playing-card money was a type of currency in Canada. The money truly was a deck of cards with the governor's signature on the back of each one.

MONEY

FACT

Canada and the U.S. are not the only countries that use the dollar as currency. Australia, Jamaica, and New Zealand have dollar bills too.

Two types of checks

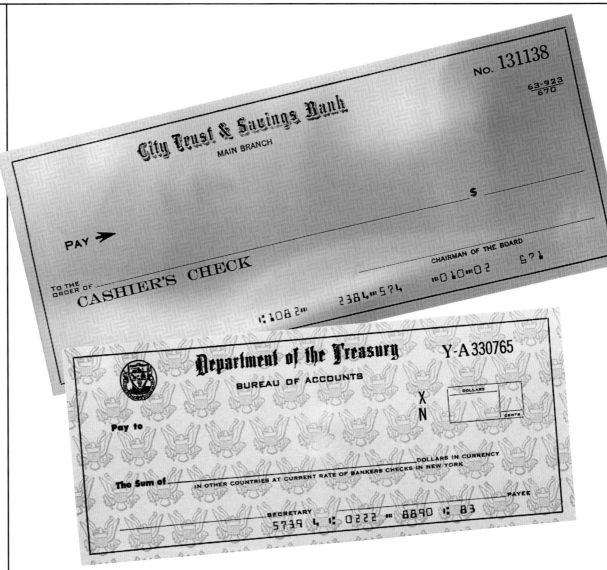

Once a month the credit card company will send a **statement** to the card holder listing all the things that he or she bought and will have to pay for. The card holder can pay the company back by writing a **check** and putting it in the mail. The check tells the card holder's bank how much money to pay to the credit card company.

S ome people don't even bother to write a check. They can have the money automatically taken out of their account by computers. Others have special software on their computers so they can do all their banking at home. Not only can they pay bills with their computer, they can get **loans** or move money around from one account to another—all without ever leaving home!

On the back of a U.S. one dollar bill is an eagle representing America's 13 original colonies. One claw holds 13 arrows, the other holds an olive branch with 13 leaves. There are also 13 stars over the eagle's head.

Cash register drawer

MONEY
FUNERAL

In the United States, worn out currency is returned to a Federal Reserve Bank where it is shredded up and burned.

Silver bar (larger) and silver ingot (smaller)

This invisible money is becoming more and more popular. In truth, over 80 percent of all the purchases made in the United States are bought and paid for by check or credit card.

Money will always be around in one form or another, and it will continue to be exchanged all over the world. It seems consumers will be seeing less and less actual cash in the future, but there's still nothing quite like the scent and the feel of a crisp new dollar bill.

MONEY

FACT

The largest bill ever printed in the U.S. was the $100,000 bill. It was used between banks to pay each other.

MONEY

DOUBLE

The franc, a French coin, was first issued in 1360 as a gold coin. It was then reissued in 1577 as a silver coin.

Top, front and back of the U.S. Susan B. Anthony silver dollar Bottom, front and back of a 10-franc coin

Glossary

Bank notes are promises printed on paper by a bank to pay money in exchange for the note.

Bartering is trading one thing for another.

A **check** is a written order for a bank to pay a certain amount of money out of a person's account.

To **counterfeit** something, such as money, is to make a fake, or a copy, of it; a counterfeit bill is a fake bill.

Credit allows a person to borrow money from a bank or a financing company; a credit card allows a person to buy things using credit instead of cash.

Printed cash or minted coins are called **currency.**

Agreements made for money that is been borrowed and must be paid back are called **loans.**

A **medium of exchange** is something that a group of people agree is valuable and has a certain worth.

Mints are factories where coins are made.

Nuggets are lumps of valuable metal such as gold and silver.

A credit **statement** is a printed monthly record of all the purchases made on an account.

Index

Australia, 19
bank notes, 16
banks, 22, 28
bartering, 6
Canada, 8

checks, 28–30
Chinese, 10, 16, 25
collecting, 7
counterfeiting, 17, 19–21

credit, 26, 28–30
loans, 29
exchange, 22–25
Euro, 14
Germany, 26

magnetic strip, 21
medium of exchange, 9
milling, 13, 19
mint, 13, 18
nuggets, 12

piggy bank, 4
salt, 10, 12
watermark, 21